LEISURELY BREAKFASTS

A Taste of Indulgence

LEISURELY BREAKFASTS

PENNY FARRELL

RAINCOAST BOOKS

Vancouver

First published in Canada in 1995 by
Raincoast Book Distribution Ltd.
8680 Cambie Street
Vancouver, B.C. V6P 6M9
(604) 323-7100

Produced by Lansdowne Publishing Pty Ltd
Level 5, 70 George Street, Sydney 2000, Australia

Canadian Cataloguing in Publication Data

Farrell, Penny, 1965-
    Leisurely breakfasts

    (A taste of indulgence)
    Includes index.
    ISBN 1-895714-84-2

    1. Breakfasts. I. Title. II. Series.
TX733.F37 1995   641.5'2   C95-910695-2

Design: Modern Times Pty Ltd
Photographer: André Martin
Stylist: Donna Hay
Photographer: Rowan Fotheringham (cover, p.2 and p.18)
Stylist: Penny Farrell (cover, p.2 and p.18)
Typeset in Garamond on Pagemaker

Printed in Singapore by Kyodo Printing Co. Pte

Front cover: Caviar with Blinis, recipe page 19
Page 2: Fresh Fruit Poached in Sauterne Syrup, recipe page 51
Back cover: Smoked Trout and Pine Nut Salad, recipe page 87

Contents

Introduction

THE OLD saying, breakfast like a king, lunch like a prince, dine like a pauper, is said to be the secret of good health and a trim body. It makes good sense — and not only in terms of health. Nothing prepares us better for whatever the day has to deliver than a good breakfast. Mornings, after all, are the best part of the day.

In summer, breakfast provides a wonderful opportunity to sit outdoors and enjoy the sun before it gets too hot. In winter, the ultimate indulgence is breakfast in bed with the morning papers. It's a wonderful way to pamper a loved one — and you can go back to bed and enjoy it as well!

Then there are all the options in between, such as breakfast for two at a charmingly set table with the morning sun flooding in. It's a lovely way to entertain too, particularly if it ties in with some other activity. For instance, if you're lucky enough to have a view of a sporting event, such as a yacht race, a car rally or a marathon run, it's nice to share it with others over breakfast. Holiday weekends — at a house in the country or a beachside cottage — are another perfect opportunity for indulgent breakfasts shared with friends.

Because our week-day breakfasts tend to be the most routine of all meals — possibly eaten on the run and in most cases eaten within a strict time frame — it's good to really relax and give yourself the time to excel at breakfast whenever you get a chance. That means a sumptuous table — or tray — setting, maybe adorned with flowers and/or fruit as a focal point. Glassware, china and cutlery can range from eclectic and informal, to your best crystal, porcelain and silver.

Once the scene is set, let your imagination go with the food. The English dwellers in stately homes knew a thing or two about breakfast. They didn't limit themselves to toast, but went all out with legs of ham and cold fowl, as well as the more usual kedgeree, succulent kidneys with crisp bacon, and eggs cooked every way imaginable.

We have the Europeans to thank for many of the ingredients and dishes that come to mind when planning a special breakfast — truffles, brioche, frittata, prosciutto, tapenade, and many more.

A perfect breakfast is light, yet substantial. It should fuel our day, without sitting heavily in the stomach.

Freshly squeezed juices are a wonderful start: try combinations such as apple and carrot; grape juice with a dash of lime; apple, pear and lime; mango juice with crushed ice; orange and strawberry with soda water or champagne; grapefruit juice and mineral water; or watermelon and champagne.

Fruit is another fundamental of a good breakfast and it's easy to add a touch of luxury by poaching in wine or liqueur. Yogurt makes a good accompaniment, but for real quality use one of the speciality yogurts in the Greek style or better still, home-made. Try stirring through a spoonful of honey and nuts, or a swirl of puréed fruit.

Fancy breads, delectable pastries, croissants, pancakes and muffins, all provide substance — and a change from everyday fare. All of these delights can be made ahead and frozen, to be produced with minimum effort in the morning.

There is no doubt that eggs come into their own at breakfast — Truffle Eggs (page 107) have to be the ultimate luxury, but Molded Eggs Florentine (page 63) isn't far behind. A soufflé will always impress with its lightness, and quiches make great breakfast fare if you are entertaining.

While it may not be possible to reach these heights Monday to Friday it's worth thinking about what you can do to improve your usual breakfast. Many of these ideas translate to everyday use. With a little planning and advance preparation you can make everyday a special day.

Breakfast like a king, and be ready to take on the world!

THE RECIPES

Apple Galettes

14 oz (450 g) ready made puff
  pastry

TOPPING:

4 apples, peeled, cored and sliced

⅓ cup (3 oz/90 g) superfine (castor)
  sugar

½ cup (4 oz/125 g) pistachio nuts,
  chopped

ROLL OUT the puff pastry until it is ¼ inch (3 mm) thick. Cut the pastry in 4 inch (12 cm) circles. Place on greased baking sheets.

Decoratively arrange the apple slices on the pastry. Sprinkle sugar and pistachio nuts over the apples. Bake in a moderately hot oven (375°F/ 190°C/Gas Mark 5) for 20 minutes or until golden and puffed.

HINTS

- home-made puff pastry gives a tasty result and can be made ahead of time and frozen in sheets ready for use

- use the best quality cooking apples for this recipe

- for a delicious variation, try baking these lovely pastries using pears

- pistachio nuts add a beautiful contrast to this recipe, but cashews or pecan nuts are just as good for texture

Serves 6

M • E • N • U
•
Fruit Platter
•
*Brioche with
Poached Eggs
(page 15)*
•
Apple Galettes
•

Apricot Almond Cake

4 oz (125 g) butter
½ cup (3½ oz/100 g) superfine
 (caster) sugar
2 eggs
1 cup (4 oz/125 g) self-rising
 (raising) flour
1 cup (5½ oz/170 g) dried apricots,
 chopped
½ cup (3 oz/90 g) sun-dried seedless
 raisins
½ cup (3 oz/90 g) dried figs, chopped
1 cup (5 oz/150 g) blanched
 almonds, roughly chopped
1 teaspoon mixed spice
½ cup (4 fl oz/125 ml) apricot
 liqueur

GREASE and line a 4 x 9 inch (10 x 20 cm) loaf pan with non-stick parchment (baking paper).

Cream the butter and sugar until light and fluffy, add the eggs and mix well. Fold in the flour, fruit, nuts, spice, and half the liqueur. Spoon the mixture into the prepared pan. Bake in a warm oven (275°F/140°C/Gas Mark 1) for 2 hours or until a wooden skewer inserted in the middle comes out clean. Remove from the oven and pour over the remaining liquid while still hot. Leave the cake to cool in the pan.

Wrap the cake tightly in plastic (cling) wrap and then in foil and store it in the refrigerator for at least 1 day (the cake will keep for up to a month, but add a little extra liqueur if storing for a long time).

Makes 1 cake

M • E • N • U
•
*Toasted Pecan Nut
Muesli with Maple Syrup
(page 101)*
•
Apricot Almond Cake
•
*Salmon Gravlax with
Caper Tapenade Style
Sauce (page 81)*
•
Cheese and Fruit
•
Apricot Almond Cake
can be baked well in
advance if necessary and
can be toasted, broiled
(grilled) or warmed in
the oven.
•

Brioche with Poached Eggs

BRIOCHE
¾ oz (20 g) compressed yeast
½ cup (4 fl oz/125 ml) warm milk
¼ cup (1 ¾ oz/50 g) superfine
   (caster) sugar
2 cups (8 oz/250 g) all-purpose
   (plain) flour
2 eggs

2 oz (60 g) butter, softened
1 egg yolk, extra
GLAZE
2 egg yolks
pinch salt
FOR SERVING
4 poached eggs
4 tomatoes, broiled (grilled)

M • E • N • U
•
Brioche with
Poached Eggs
•
Strawberries in
Strawberry Liqueur
(page 91)
•
Yogurt
•

Poached eggs must
always be prepared at the
last minute — leaving
them to stand will
toughen the eggs.
•

CREAM the yeast with the sugar and a little milk. Add the remaining milk and let the mixture stand in a warm place for 10 minutes or until it is frothy.

Sift the flour into a bowl; add the eggs and the yeast mixture. Mix well. Add half the butter and beat the dough until it is smooth. Dot the remaining butter over the top of the dough, then cover and let stand in a warm place for 40 minutes or until it is doubled in size.

Beat the dough until it doesn't stick to the sides of the bowl. Freeze for 15 minutes. Knead the dough on a lightly floured board until it is smooth. Whisk together the glaze ingredients. Shape the dough into 8 large balls and 8 small balls. Place the large balls in 8 individual brioche or fluted molds, brush with a little glaze, and place the smaller balls on top. Cover them lightly and let stand in a warm place for 40 minutes or until they are doubled in size.

Brush the brioche with remaining glaze and bake in a hot oven (400°F/200°C/Gas Mark 6) for 25 minutes or until they are deep golden and sound hollow when tapped on top.

Serves 4

Butterscotch Pancakes

BUTTERSCOTCH SAUCE
¼ cup (2 oz/60 g) cultured butter
½ cup (4 oz/125 g) packed (soft)
    brown sugar
4 teaspoons Marsala liqueur
⅓ cup (2¾ fl oz/80 ml) heavy
    (double) cream

PANCAKES
1 cup (4 oz/125 g) self-rising
    (raising) flour

1 teaspoon double-acting baking
    powder (2 teaspoons baking powder)
½ cup (4 oz/125 g) packed (soft)
    brown sugar
1 egg
1¼ cups (10 fl oz/300 ml) milk
¾ oz (20 g) butter, melted
extra butter, for cooking
heavy (double) cream, whipped

M • E • N • U
•
Poached Trout with Dill
Mayonnaise
(page 75)
•
Butterscotch Pancakes
•
Caffe Latté
•

IN A small saucepan, melt the butter over a medium heat until it is just beginning to turn golden. Add the brown sugar and cook for 2 minutes. Reduce heat, then add the Marsala and cream. Continue cooking until the butterscotch thickens slightly, but do not let it boil. Remove from the heat and leave to stand at room temperature until required.

Make the pancake batter by sifting the flour and baking powder into a bowl. Add the sugar. In a separate bowl, combine the egg, milk and melted butter. Stir this mixture into the dry ingredients and whisk until no lumps of flour remain. Cover and refrigerate the batter for 30 minutes.

Heat a 6 inch (15 cm) crepe or omelet pan over a medium heat. Add a little butter and when melted, pour in approximately ⅓ cup (2¾ fl oz/80 ml) of the batter. Cook the pancake until it is golden on both sides. As the pancakes cook place them on an ovenproof dish in a warm oven and cover them with foil. Serve with cooled butterscotch sauce and cream.

Serves 4

Caviar with Blinis

CRÈME FRAICHE

1 cup (8 fl oz/250 ml) heavy
    (double) cream

1 tablespoon yogurt

BLINIS

⅓ oz (10 g) compressed yeast

1 tablespoon superfine (caster) sugar

1 cup (8 fl oz/250 ml) lukewarm
    milk

¾ cup (3 oz/90 g) buckwheat flour

¾ cup (3 oz/90 g) all-purpose
    (plain) flour

2 eggs

2 oz (60 g) butter, melted

extra butter, for cooking

FOR SERVING

4 oz (125 g) caviar (Beluga or
    Iranian)

2 eggs, hard-cooked (hard-boiled)

chives, chopped

MAKE the Crème Fraiche by combining the cream and yogurt. Leave to stand at room temperature for 24–36 hours or until it is thick (this standing time will vary according to climate).

To make the blinis, cream the yeast with the sugar and a little milk. Add the remaining milk and stir well. Place the mixture in a warm position for 10 minutes or until it is frothy.

Whisk in the flours, eggs and butter. Stand for 30 minutes in a warm position. Heat a small crepe pan and cook tablespoons of the batter in butter on both sides until golden.

Serve caviar with Crème Fraiche, blinis, chopped egg and chives.

Serves 4

M • E • N • U

•

Caviar with Blinis

•

*Smoked Trout and Pine
Nut Salad
(page 87)*

•

*Exotic Summer Fruit
Medley with
Macadamia Toffee
(page 43)*

Good quality caviar will
store in the refrigerator
for months so this
breakfast can become a
great standby for a
special occasion.

•

Cheese and Corn Bread Rolls

½ oz (15 g) compressed yeast
1 cup (8 fl oz/250 ml) warm milk
1 teaspoon sea salt
2 tablespoons (1½ fl oz/45 ml) light
    corn (golden) syrup
2 tablespoons (1½ fl oz/45 ml) good
    quality olive oil
1 teaspoon bread improver

½ cup (2½ oz/75 g) fine corn
    meal (polenta)
3 cups (12 oz/375 g) unbleached all-
    purpose (plain) flour
1 oz (30 g) Parmesan cheese, grated
2 egg yolks, beaten
1 tablespoon polenta (fine corn meal)
1 tablespoon Parmesan cheese, grated

CREAM the yeast with the milk. Mix in the salt, corn syrup and oil. Set aside for 10 minutes or until it is frothy or creamy-looking on top.

Sift the bread improver, corn meal, and flour into a bowl. Add the yeast mixture and cheese and mix to a manageable dough. Knead the dough thoroughly for 10 minutes or until it is smooth and elastic. Cover and place in a warm position for 40 minutes or until the dough has doubled in size.

Brush the insides of six 3¼ x 4 inch (8 x 10 cm) unglazed terracotta pots or baby loaf pans thoroughly with olive oil.

Punch down the bread dough and divide it into 6 equal portions. Knead each portion lightly, then place it in a pot or pan. Place in a warm position for 40 minutes or until the rolls are well risen and nicely shaped. Brush the top of each roll with egg yolk then sprinkle with corn meal and cheese. Bake in a moderately hot oven (400°F/200°C/Gas Mark 6) for 30 minutes or until the bread is cooked and sounds hollow when tapped on top.

Makes 6 individual breads

M • E • N • U
•
Melon Slices
•
Cheese and Corn
Bread Rolls
•
Salami and Cooked Sliced
Meats with
Marinated Vegetables
(Eggplant, Capsicum,
Tomatoes, Olives etc)
•
Melon slices are a
delicate start and can be
served throughout the
meal as an
accompaniment.
•

Cheese Soufflés

2 oz (60 g) butter
⅓ cup (1½ oz/45 g) all-purpose
(plain) flour
2 cups (16 fl oz/500 ml) milk
½ cup (2 oz/60 g) mature cheddar
cheese, grated
½ cup (2 oz/60 g) smoked cheese,
grated
4 eggs, separated

PLACE the butter in a saucepan over a low heat and stir until melted.

Add the flour and cook for one minute, stirring all the time.

Remove from the heat and gradually whisk in the milk making sure there are no lumps. Return to the heat and stir constantly until the mixture boils and thickens.

Remove from the heat and stir the cheeses and egg yolks through the mixture.

Beat the egg whites until soft peaks form and fold through the cheese mixture. Pour into 6 individual ramekins or soufflé dishes.

Bake in a moderately hot oven (400°F /200°C/Gas Mark 6) for 25 minutes or until puffed and golden brown. Serve immediately.

Serves 6

Cherry Muffins

4 oz (125 g) mascarpone cheese
½ cup (3½ oz/100 g) demerara sugar
1 egg
2 cups (8 oz/250 g) self-rising
    (raising) flour
1 cup (8 fl oz/250 ml) milk

8 oz (250 g) fresh pitted cherries or
    13½ oz (425 g) can pitted
    cherries, drained and halved
2 tablespoons demerara sugar, extra
cherries, extra
mascarpone, extra

BEAT the mascarpone and sugar until creamy (the sugar does not dissolve so the mixture will be granular). Add the egg and continue beating until it is thoroughly mixed in.

Sift the flour and lightly fold into the egg mixture with the cherries and milk. Mix only until just combined — do not overmix.

Spoon the mixture into a greased 12-cup muffin pan. Sprinkle with extra sugar. Bake in a moderate oven (350°F/180°C/Gas Mark 4) for 40 minutes or until cooked. Serve the muffins warm with extra fresh cherries and mascarpone.

Makes 12

M • E • N • U
•
*Freshly Squeezed Orange
Juice*
•
*Homemade Sausages
with Onions
(page 59)*
•
Cherry Muffins
•
To gain the most benefit from the orange juice, it must be squeezed at the last minute.
•

Chervil Frittata

2 oz (60 g) butter
2 bacon strips (rashers), fat and rind
    removed, diced
1 red bell pepper (capsicum), seeded
    and diced
8 eggs
½ cup (4 fl oz/125 ml) Crème
    Fraiche (page 19) or light
    sour cream

chervil sprigs
sea salt, to taste
freshly ground pepper, to taste
1 cup (5 oz/150 g) vintage cheddar
    cheese, grated

M • E • N • U
•
Chervil Frittata
•
*Olive and Sun-dried
Tomato Bread*
(page 67)
•
Fresh Berries
•

Standing tends to toughen
the eggs, so remember if
you are serving the frittata
cold, undercook rather
than overcook it.

•

HEAT a 9½ in (24 cm) frying pan over a medium flame. If possible use a non-stick or well-seasoned frying pan with a heavy base and, preferably, a metal handle. Melt the butter and sauté the bacon and bell pepper until the bacon begins to become crisp. Reduce the heat to a low heat and cook for a further 2 minutes.

In a bowl, whisk together the eggs, Crème Fraiche, half the chervil, salt and pepper. Pour over the bacon and bell pepper and cook over a low heat for 5–8 minutes until nearly set.

Sprinkle over the remaining chervil and all of the cheese. Place the saucepan under a hot broiler (grill) (protecting the pan handle if it is not metallic) and broil until the frittata is completely set and the cheese top is golden, about 5 minutes. Serve warm or cold, cut into wedges.

Serves 4

Chicken and Pistachio Roll

1 double chicken breast

STUFFING

4 oz (125 g) chicken livers, chopped
finely

4 oz (125 g) veal, ground finely

1 small onion, minced

2 cloves of garlic, minced

grated peel (rind) of 1 orange

1 cup (6 oz/150 g) pistachio nuts,
   chopped

1 egg white

salt and pepper

MIX together all the stuffing ingredients. Place the chicken skin down on
a work bench. Mound the stuffing along the middle of the chicken.

Roll the chicken up into a sausage shape and secure with kitchen
twine. Place in a shallow baking pan and bake in a moderate oven
(350°F/180°C/Gas Mark 4) for 1 hour or until the juices run yellow
when a skewer is inserted. Remove from the oven and serve sliced either
hot or cold.

Serves 4

Chicken Crepes with Basil Mayonnaise

1 egg
1¼ cups (10 fl oz/300 ml) milk
1 tablespoon (¾ oz/20 g) butter,
    melted
2 teaspoons Dijon mustard
1 cup (4 oz/125 g) all-purpose
    (plain) flour, sifted
4 chicken thigh fillets, trimmed

1 cup (8 fl oz/250 ml) strong chicken
    stock
2 teaspoons pickled pink peppercorns
½ cup (4 fl oz/125 ml) light (single)
    cream
2 tablespoons sun-dried tomatoes,
    sliced
2 teaspoons tomato paste (passato)
Basil Mayonnaise, for serving

BEAT together the egg, milk, butter and mustard. Whisk the liquid into the flour until no lumps of flour remain. Cover and refrigerate for 30 minutes.

Place the chicken fillets in a shallow pan with the stock and peppercorns. Simmer for 5 minutes or until chicken is cooked, turning the fillets over occasionally. Turn the heat off and allow the fillets to rest in the stock for 5 minutes. Remove the chicken and thinly slice. Cook the stock over a high heat until reduced to almost nothing, then add the cream, tomatoes, tomato paste and chicken slices. Simmer over the lowest possible heat until required.

Heat a 6 inch (15 cm) crepe or omelet pan over a medium heat. Add a little butter, then enough pancake batter to make a small crepe. Cook the pancakes until golden on both sides. Cover with foil and place in a warm oven until required. Fold the pancakes in half, place the chicken in the middle and serve with Basil Mayonnaise.

Serves 4

BASIL MAYONNAISE

•

2 egg yolks
1 teaspoon lemon juice
½ cup (4 fl oz/125 ml)
    light olive oil
2 teaspoons hot chicken
    stock
10 fresh basil leaves

•

Place the egg yolks in a blender and blend until pale and thick. With the motor still running, first add the lemon juice and then add the oil, in a very slow, steady stream — this process will take 5 minutes. Add the chicken stock and basil leaves and blend well.

•

Chilled Mango Soufflé

3 teaspoons (1 sachet) gelatin
¼ cup (2 fl oz/60 ml) mango
    liqueur
3 eggs, separated
½ cup (6½ oz/200 g) superfine
    (caster) sugar
8 oz (250 g) fresh ricotta cheese

1 cup (8 fl oz/250 ml) heavy
    (double) cream, whipped
1 cup (8 fl oz/250 ml) fresh mango
    purée
½ cup (3 oz/90 g) shelled, unsalted
    pistachio nuts, crushed

M • E • N • U
•
Apple Galettes
(page 11)
•
Grilled Roma Tomatoes
with Prosciutto
(page 55)
•
Chilled Mango Soufflé
•

TIE A sheet of parchment (baking paper) securely around a soufflé or other straight-sided dish.

Combine the gelatin and mango liqueur in a small bowl. Place the bowl over boiling water, and heat until dissolved. Remove from the heat and cool.

Beat the egg yolks with the sugar until thick and pale. Add the ricotta and beat until smooth. In a separate bowl, beat the egg whites until stiff.

Combine the ricotta mixture, egg whites, whipped cream, mango purée and gelatin. Pour into the prepared dish and sprinkle the pistachio nuts over the top. Refrigerate for 3 hours or until required.

Serves 4–6

Chilled Shrimp (Prawn) Mousseline

12 oz (375 g) shelled green shrimp
    (prawn) meat
3 egg whites
sea salt, to taste
freshly ground red peppercorns, to
    taste

2 cups (1 lb/500 g) light (single)
    cream (35% fat content), well
    chilled
Melba toasts, for serving
dill or chervil sprigs, for garnish

PLACE the shrimp in a blender and purée. Add the egg whites and salt and pepper and blend until smooth. Leave the mixture in the blender jug and place it in the coldest part of the refrigerator for 30 minutes.

Return the blender jug to the machine, and with the motor running add the cream. Return to the refrigerator for 30–40 minutes (if time permits, leave the mixture there for 1–2 hours).

Grease 6 individual soufflé dishes. Spoon the mousseline mixture into each soufflé dish, then sit the soufflé dishes in a baking dish. Pour hot water into the baking dish, allowing the water to rise halfway up the sides of the soufflé dishes.

Bake the Shrimp Mousseline at 350°F (180°C/Gas Mark 4) for 12–15 minutes or until it is firm to touch. Remove from the oven and the waterbath. Cool slightly, cover and refrigerate for 2 hours or until required.

Unmold the Mousseline and serve with Melba toasts and sprigs of dill or chervil.

Serves 6

M • E • N • U
•
*Non-alcoholic Fruit
Cocktails*
•
*Chilled Shrimp (Prawn)
Mousseline*
•
*Pesto and Parmesan
Palmiers
(page 73)*
•

To make the cocktails, simply blend fresh fruits with either lots of ice or milk. Serve well chilled and garnished with the appropriate fruit.
•

Coffee Granita

1 cup (6½ oz/200 g) superfine (caster) sugar
½ cup (4 fl oz/125 ml) water

2 cups (16 fl oz/500 ml) very strong freshly brewed coffee

PLACE the sugar and water in a saucepan. Stir over a low heat until the sugar dissolves. Brush the sides of the saucepan with water to remove any sugar granules, then cook syrup over a low heat without stirring until it starts to turn a very pale golden around the outside of the pan. Remove from the heat and add the coffee. Place the mixture in a metal bowl and refrigerate to cool.

When cool, cover the bowl of Granita with foil and transfer to the freezer. Freeze the Granita for 4–5 hours stirring every half hour to break up the ice crystals (it may take a little longer to freeze, depending on the freezer).

NOTE: To vary the Granita, change the blend of coffee beans. Once frozen, the Granita can be stored in the freezer for 24 hours. If storing for longer, the Granita should be mixed daily. It must be eaten within a week.

Serves 2–4

Croissants with Fresh Strawberry Jam

⅓ oz (10 g) compressed yeast

2 tablespoons warm water

1 tablespoon superfine (caster) sugar

1 cup (4 oz/125 g) all-purpose
  (plain) flour

½ teaspoon salt

⅓ cup (3 fl oz/90 ml) warm milk

1 tablespoon light olive oil

2 oz (60 g) butter, softened

Strawberry Jam, for serving

CREAM the yeast with the water and sugar. Sift the flour and salt and add the yeast, milk and oil. Mix to a dough, then knead for 10 minutes until smooth.

Place the dough in an oiled bowl, cover and stand in a warm position for 40 minutes or until it has doubled in size. Knock down the dough and knead it until it is smooth. Roll the dough out to form a rectangle. Cover and allow the dough to double in size as before. Chill for 30 minutes.

Place the dough on a floured board. Spread butter over the closest ⅔ of the dough, leaving a ½ inch (1 cm) border around the edge. Fold the closest ⅓ of dough over the middle, then fold the top ⅓ over this. Roll out and repeat the folding process. Chill for 10 minutes. Fold, roll and chill another two times.

Roll the dough out to 8 x 4 inches (20 x 10 cm). Cut it into 3 rectangles, then cut each in half diagonally. Starting at the base of each triangle, roll up towards the point, then curve each roll into a crescent shape and place on a greased baking sheet. Cover and allow to double in size as before.

Bake in a fairly hot oven (425°F/220°C/Gas Mark 7) for 12–15 minutes or until golden. Serve warm with Strawberry Jam.

Makes 6 croissants

STRAWBERRY JAM

•

1 lb (500 g) fresh
strawberries, hulled

1 lb (500 g) sugar

grated peel (rind) and juice
2 lemons

•

Place the strawberries, sugar, lemon peel and juice in a heavy-based saucepan. Bring to a boil stirring constantly, then reduce heat and simmer uncovered for approximately 40 minutes or until the consistency of thick jam. Transfer to a bowl and cool.

•

Duck with Citrus Sauce

2 duck breasts
2 oz (60 g) butter
1 cup (8 oz/250 ml) orange juice
1 orange
1 tablespoon sugar
2 teaspoons vinegar

2 cups (16 oz/500 ml) water
2 chicken stock cubes
2 teaspoons lemon juice
salt and pepper, to taste
1 teaspoon cornstarch (cornflour)

RUB THE duck breasts with butter and place in a shallow baking pan with half of the orange juice. Roast in a moderate oven (350°F/180°C/Gas Mark 4) for 20–35 minutes. Baste the duck breasts occasionally with the juices in the pan.

Remove the peel (rind) from the orange, taking care to cut off all the white pith. Cut the peel into strips.

Combine all the remaining ingredients, except the cornstarch, in a saucepan with the orange peel and bring to a boil. Boil rapidly until the sauce has reduced by half. Strain the sauce and return it to the saucepan, add salt and pepper. Stir a tablespoon of the hot liquid into the cornstarch and when smooth pour it into the simmering sauce. Stir over a medium heat until thickened.

To serve slice the duck breasts and pour over the sauce.

Serves 2–4

Exotic Summer Fruit Medley with Macadamia Toffee

2 lb (1 kg) fresh exotic summer fruits (eg figs, raspberries, corella pears, nectarines, dates, cherries, blood plums, gooseberries, melon balls, mango, papaya, pink guava), cut into bite size pieces and all seeds removed

¼ cup (2½ oz/75 ml) fresh lime juice

1 cup (8 oz/250 g) country style yogurt

MACADAMIA TOFFEE

½ cup (2¾ oz/80 g) macadamia nuts, unsalted

⅔ cup (5 oz/150 g) sugar

2 fl oz (60 ml/¼ cup) water

PLACE prepared fruit in a serving bowl. Pour over lime juice, cover and refrigerate until required.

Roast nuts at 350°F (180°C/Gas Mark 4) for 10 minutes or until just golden. Place on a non-stick baking tray.

Heat sugar and water in a heavy based saucepan, stirring constantly until the sugar dissolves. Brush some water around the sides of the saucepan to remove any excess sugar crystals, then cook syrup, without stirring, until it becomes a toffee colour (this process will take approximately 5 minutes, but do not leave it alone as the time can vary considerably).

Pour toffee over nuts and allow to harden. When cold, break toffee into bite size pieces. Sprinkle over Fruit Medley and serve with yogurt.

Serves 4–6

M • E • N • U
•
Champagne Cocktails
•
Exotic Summer Fruit Medley with Macadamia Toffee
•
Cheese Platter
•
Use good quality French champagne or sparkling wine for champagne cocktails. Any liqueur or fruit purée can be added to the champagne.
•

Figs in Port with Mascarpone

12 fresh figs
½ cup (4 fl oz/125 ml) vintage port
¼ cup (1¾ oz/50 g) demerara
  sugar

1 cup (8 oz/250 g) mascarpone
  cheese

CUT THE figs in half lengthways. Place them in a shallow container cut side up and pour over the port. Allow to marinate for at least 30 minutes, or until required.

Line a broil (grill) tray with foil. Place the figs on the tray, cut side up, reserving any leftover port. Sprinkle with the sugar and broil (grill) until the sugar begins to brown. Serve the figs hot or cold with mascarpone cheese. Pour any leftover port over the figs before serving.

Serves 2–4

M • E • N • U
•
*Sun-dried Bell Pepper
(Capsicum) Tartlets
(page 93)*
•
*Figs in Port with
Mascarpone*
•
Iced Coffee
•

Fish Roll-ups with Butter Sauce

4 fillets of white fish, skinned and
  boned
7 fl oz (210 ml) of dry vermouth
26 fl oz (800 ml) water
SAUCE
3 egg yolks

1 tablespoon of lime juice
8 oz (250 g) butter
1 teaspoon lime peel (rind), grated
16 snow peas (mangetout), for
serving
red caviar, for serving

Cheese and Parsley Puffs

ROLL UP fillets and secure with toothpicks starting at the thin end of each
fillet. Mix vermouth and water in a flat round pan and bring to the boil.
Stand rolls on end in boiling liquid and reduce heat until liquid is only
just simmering. Cook for about 4 or 5 minutes or until fish is cooked.
Remove rolls from liquid, drain on paper towels and keep in a warm place.

To make the sauce place egg yolks in a blender with the lime juice.
Heat the butter until hot and bubbling but not brown. Set blender to a
low speed and slowly pour in hot butter and blend until smooth. Add lime
peel. Serve the dish immediately while sauce is still hot.

To serve place a Fish Roll-up on each plate. Pour sauce over the top.
Serve with snow peas, red caviar and Cheese and Parsley Puffs.

Serves 4

CHEESE AND PARSLEY
PUFFS

•

4 sheets of ready rolled puff
pastry
6 oz (180 g) gorgonzola
1¼ cup (4 oz/125 g) freshly
chopped parsley
1 egg, lightly beaten

•

Mold cheese into 18 stick
shaped portions. Cut
pastry into 3 x 3 inch (8 x
8 cm) squares. Place
cheese sticks in middle of
squares and sprinkle with
parsley. Put another
square on top and press
edges together. Bake in a
hot oven (400°F/200°C/
Gas Mark 6) for 15
minutes or until golden
brown.

•

French Toast

2 eggs
½ cup (4 fl oz/125 g) light (single)
　　cream
½ teaspoon cinnamon
1 tablespoon sugar

8 slices brioche (page 15)
1 tablespoon (¾ oz/20 g) butter
maple syrup, for serving
cinnamon and confectioners' (icing)
　　sugar, for serving

PLACE eggs, cream, cinnamon and sugar in a shallow bowl and whisk to combine.

Soak brioche in egg mixture for 15 seconds each side.

Heat the butter in a frying pan over a moderate heat. When the butter is foaming place the brioche in the pan and cook for 3 minutes each side or until golden. Serve with maple syrup and dust with extra cinnamon and confectioners' sugar.

Serves 4

M • E • N • U
•
French Toast
•
Parmesan Roulade with
Smoked Salmon
(page 71)
•
Tarte Tatin
(page 99)
•

Fresh Fruit Poached in Sauterne Syrup

12 fl oz (375 ml) Sauterne or sweet
   white wine
½ cup (3½ oz/100 g) superfine
   (caster) sugar

2 lb (1 kg) ripe fresh fruit — eg
   peaches, pears, tamarillos
water

PLACE the Sauterne and sugar in a saucepan. Bring to a boil, stirring occasionally to dissolve the sugar.

Place the fruit in the syrup and add sufficient water to cover it. Simmer for 10 minutes or until the fruit is just tender. Remove the fruit from the syrup; peel any skins that need removing and cut any large fruit in half.

Continue cooking the Sauterne syrup over a high heat until it is reduced and syrupy. Cool before serving over the fruit.

Serves 4

M • E • N • U
•
Watermelon Slices
•
Tarte à L'Oignon
(page 97)
•
Fresh Fruit Poached in
Sauterne Syrup
•
Serve the Fresh Fruit
Poached in Sauterne
Syrup in a beautiful big
bowl so it becomes the
feature of the meal.
•

Fruit Jelly

ORANGE JELLY

½ cup (3½ oz/100 g) superfine
  (caster) sugar
6 large oranges, juiced
2 teaspoons powdered gelatin
¼ cup (2 fl oz/60 ml) orange
  liqueur
1 drop orange food coloring,
  optional

ORANGE CREAM

finely grated peel (rind) 3 oranges
8 oz (250 g) cream cheese or
  Neufchatel
¼ cup (1¾ oz/50 g) superfine
  (caster) sugar
1 tablespoon orange liqueur
4 oranges
orange peel (rind), cut in julienne

PLACE the sugar and 2 tablespoons of orange juice in a small saucepan.
Cook over a medium heat until the sugar dissolves, stirring constantly.
Remove from the heat and stir in the gelatin, making sure all lumps are
removed. Add the remaining orange juice and the orange liqueur. If the
orange mixture is too pale, add some orange food coloring. Lightly grease a
4 cup (32 fl oz/1 L) capacity mold. Pour the orange mixture into the
mold, lightly cover and refrigerate for 2 hours or until required.

Beat all the ingredients for the Orange Cream with an electric mixer
until smooth. Refrigerate until required.

Cut the top and bottom from the oranges. Stand one orange on its base
and carefully cut away all the skin and pith. Carefully cut between the
membranes of the orange to release the individual segments. Repeat with
the remaining oranges.

Unmold the Fruit Jelly and serve with Orange Cream, orange segments
and garnish with julienne strips of orange peel.

Serves 4

M • E • N • U
•
Fruit Jelly
•
English Muffin Pizzas
•
Make quick pizzas
using English Muffins
and your desired toppings.
Simply broil (grill)
until cheese melts.
•

Grilled Roma Tomatoes with Prosciutto

12 Roma tomatoes (Roman
    tomatoes, egg tomatoes or Italian
    tomatoes)
2 tablespoons (1½ fl oz/45 ml)
    extra virgin olive oil
2 oz (60 g) herbed chèvre
    (goat cheese)

2 teaspoons capers
sea salt, to taste
ground gourmet peppercorns, to taste
12 slices prosciutto, fat removed

CUT the tomatoes in half lengthways. Brush them lightly with oil. Place a sheet of foil over the broiler (grill) plate; arrange the tomatoes on it and broil them under a low heat until just cooked but still firm enough to handle (about 5 minutes) turning occasionally.

Spread a little chèvre on the cut side of each tomato. Top with the capers, and season to taste with salt and pepper. Wrap a slice of prosciutto around each tomato half, securing with a toothpick if necessary. Brush with any remaining oil.

Return the tomatoes to the broiler and cook until the prosciutto becomes crisp, approximately 3–4 minutes.

NOTE: Gourmet peppercorns include dried red, green, white and black peppercorns

Serves 6

M • E • N • U
•
Fresh Apricots with Cottage Cheese
•
Grilled Roma Tomatoes with Prosciutto
•

To make a simple healthy starter, cut the apricots in half, remove the seeds (stones) and fill with cottage cheese.
•

Hazelnut Shortbread

½ cup (3 oz/90 g) hazelnuts, roasted
  and skinned
4 oz (125 g) unsalted butter
⅓ cup (2 oz/60 g) superfine (caster)
  sugar
2 cups (8 oz/250 g) all-purpose
  (plain) flour

2 tablespoons (1½ fl oz/45 ml) milk
2 tablespoons superfine (caster)
  sugar, extra
fresh fruit, for serving

M • E • N • U
•
Basket of Berries
•
*Chicken Crepes with Basil
Mayonnaise
(page 31)*
•
Hazelnut Shortbread
•

PLACE the hazelnuts in a food processor or blender and process until they are very fine. Add the butter and sugar and process until creamed. With the processor going, gradually add sufficient flour to form a manageable dough.

Remove the shortbread from processor bowl and lightly knead until the mixture is well combined. Shape the shortbread into an even round shape, about ½ inch (1½ cm) thick. Transfer to a greased baking sheet. Crimp the edges of the shortbread and cut divisions on the top of the dough, making sure you don't cut through to the base.

Cover and refrigerate the shortbread for at least an hour.

Brush with milk and sprinkle with the extra superfine sugar. Bake in a moderate oven (350°F/180°C/Gas Mark 4) for 30 minutes or until golden and crisp. Cool the shortbread on the baking sheet and serve broken into wedges with fresh fruit.

Serves 4

Homemade Sausages with Onions

1 pork sausage casing
1 lb (500 g) pork fillet, ground
    (minced)
8 oz (250 g) pancetta, ground
    (minced)
1–2 teaspoons salt

1 teaspoon gourmet peppercorns
2 large onions, very thinly sliced
2 tablespoons (1½ oz/45 g) butter
2 tablespoons olive oil
toast, for serving

M • E • N • U
•
Fresh Fruit Juice
•
Homemade Sausages with
Onions
•
Butterscotch Pancakes
(page 17)
•

SOAK the pork sausage casing in water for 10 minutes. Remove and dry thoroughly.

Combine the sausage ingredients. Using a large piping bag fitted with a plain wide nozzle, pipe the sausage mixture into the casing. Make sure you don't leave any large pockets of air, but do not over-stuff.

Tie a knot at one end of the pork casing, then twist the casing into individual sausages at 1–1½ inch (3–4 cm) intervals. Hang the sausage in a well-ventilated area for 1–2 hours or until the casing is very dry. Refrigerate until required (the sausages must be eaten within 3 days as they contain no preservative).

Sauté the onions in butter and oil over a low flame for 10–15 minutes or until the onions have caramelized. Cut the sausages into individual portions and add to the pan. Cook a further 10–15 minutes or until the sausages are cooked through, adding extra butter and oil if required. Serve Sausages with Onions with lots of toast.

Serves 4

Lobster Medallion Benedict

HOLLANDAISE SAUCE
2 egg yolks
1 tablespoon lemon juice
4 oz (125 g) butter, finely diced
EGGS BENEDICT
1 lobster (crayfish) tail, cooked and
shelled, warmed

water, for poaching
1 tablespoon white vinegar
4 eggs
4 thick slices bread or English
muffins

PLACE the egg yolks, lemon juice and butter in the top of a double boiler over simmering water. Whisk the egg until slightly thickened. Add the butter one piece at a time, whisking constantly until all the butter has been incorporated and the Hollandaise is thick, creamy and perfectly smooth.

Cut the lobster into 4–8 medallions, depending on the size of the lobster.

Place a large frying pan of water over a high heat (the water should be deep enough to cover an egg). Bring the water to a boil and add the vinegar, reduce the heat so the water is only just simmering. Crack an egg onto a plate. Gently slide the egg off the plate into the water, then repeat with remaining eggs. Cook uncovered for 3–5 minutes, depending how you like your eggs cooked.

Serve toasted bread or muffins with a medallion of lobster, an egg on top and Hollandaise sauce.

NOTE: If the sauce overheats, immediately place the top of the double boiler over cold water and put an ice cube and an extra egg yolk in the sauce. This should bring the sauce back to its correct consistency.

Serves 4

M • E • N • U
•
Poached Pears
•
Lobster Medallion Benedict
•
Queen Style Pudding
(page 77)
•

Lobster Medallion Benedict served with Champagne is the perfect combination for a special occasion.
•

Molded Eggs Florentine

1 bunch English spinach
1 tablespoon hazelnut oil
½ teaspoon nutmeg, freshly grated
sea salt, to taste
freshly ground black pepper, to taste

1 tablespoon (¾ oz/20 g) butter
4 eggs
2 tablespoons roasted red bell pepper
    (capsicum), skinned and chopped
toast, for serving

WASH the spinach thoroughly and discard most of the stems. Roughly chop the spinach and place it in a frying pan with the oil. Cook over a high heat until the spinach has wilted and nearly all the liquid has evaporated. Transfer the spinach to a sieve and drain it thoroughly, pressing down firmly with the back of a spoon. Season with the nutmeg, salt and pepper and add the butter. Divide between 4 well greased ¾ cup capacity heatproof ramekins.

Break an egg into each ramekin and top with bell pepper. Cover each ramekin securely with foil, then place in a deep frying pan with hot water reaching halfway up the side of the ramekins. Cover the frying pan and steam the Eggs Florentine for 4 minutes or until they're cooked to your desire. Serve immediately with toast.

Serves 4

M • E • N • U
•
Roasted Cashew Nuts
•
Molded Eggs Florentine
•
Fresh Bread Rolls
•

Hot roasted cashew nuts are a great starter for any breakfast. The smell stimulates the tastebuds and they are not filling.
•

Mushrooms Stuffed with Crab and Mirepoix of Vegetables

6 very large, flat field mushrooms
1 small carrot, peeled and finely
  chopped
1 stick celery, peeled and finely
  chopped
½ red bell pepper (capsicum),
  seeded and finely chopped
2 tablespoons chopped chives

2 oz (60 g) butter
½ cup (4 oz/125 g) fresh crab meat
  (preferably mud crab or sand
  crab)
½ cup (1 oz/30 g) fresh
  breadcrumbs
2 tablespoons grated Parmesan cheese
2 tablespoons (1½ oz/45 g) melted butter

REMOVE the stems from the mushrooms. Finely chop the stems and combine with the carrot, celery, pepper and chives.

Heat the butter in a large frying pan. Cook the mushrooms with the stem side up for 2–3 minutes — do not turn them over. Remove the mushrooms from the pan and transfer to a broiler (griller) tray.

Place the vegetable mixture in the frying pan and cook over a high heat for 2 minutes or until all liquid has evaporated. Combine the cooked vegetable mirepoix with the crab meat and use to stuff the mushroom cups.

Combine the breadcrumbs, cheese and melted butter. Sprinkle over the stuffed mushrooms and broil (grill) under a low heat for 2 minutes or until golden.

Serves 3–6

M • E • N • U
•
Mushrooms Stuffed with
Crab and Mirepoix of
Vegetables
•
Cheese Soufflés
(page 23)
•
Strawberries in Strawberry
Liqueur
(page 91)
•
Mushrooms must be
cooked at the last minute
or they will loose their
texture.
•

Olive and Sun-dried Tomato Bread

¾ oz (20 g) compressed yeast
1 tablespoon superfine (caster) sugar
2 tablespoons (1½ oz/45 g) butter,
   softened
½ cup (4 fl oz/125 ml) warm milk
1 egg
1½ cups (6 oz/185 g) all-purpose
   (plain) flour

½ teaspoon salt
3 oz (90 g) sun-dried tomatoes,
   sliced
3 oz (90 g) pitted large black olives,
   sliced
10–12 leaves of fresh basil, chopped

M • E • N • U
•
Olive and Sun-dried
Tomato Bread
•
Avocados with Vinaigrette
•
Chicken and Pistachio Roll
(page 29)
•

CREAM the yeast with the sugar and butter. Stir in the milk and egg, cover and stand in a warm position for 10 minutes or until frothy.

Sift the flour and salt into a large bowl. Add the tomatoes, olives and basil. Pour in the yeast mixture and mix well to form a dough.

Knead the dough on a floured board for 10 minutes or until it is smooth and silky. Place in a large greased bowl. Cover and place in a warm position for 40 minutes or until the dough is doubled in size.

Knock down the dough, transfer to the floured board and knead for a few minutes or until smooth. Place in a greased 3½ x 7½ inch (9 x 19 cm) loaf pan. Lightly cover and place in a warm position for a further 40 minutes or until doubled in size.

Bake in a moderate oven (350°F/180°C/Gas Mark 4) for 50 minutes or until the bread sounds hollow when tapped. Serve hot or cold with lots of butter.

Makes 1 loaf

Oysters with Bacon and Fish Jelly

1 dozen fresh rock oysters, shucked
(opened)
2 bacon strips (rashers), fat and
rind removed
1 tablespoon olive oil

3 cups (24 fl oz/750 ml) strong-
tasting fresh fish or seafood
stock
½ teaspoon gelatin
2 teaspoons caviar (Beluga or
Iranian)

CLEAN any broken shell from the oysters, cover and refrigerate until required.

Finely chop the bacon and sauté in oil until very crisp. Drain on paper towel and set aside.

Place the stock in a saucepan. Cook over a high heat until it is reduced to ½ cup, approximately 30 minutes. Remove from the heat and stir in the gelatin, making sure no lumps remain. Transfer to a shallow container and refrigerate for 30 minutes or until set.

Mix the fish jelly with a fork, then spoon it over the oysters. Top with the bacon and serve with the caviar.

Serves 2

M • E • N • U
•
*Broiled (grilled) Ruby
Grapefruit*
•
*Oysters with Bacon
and Fish Jelly*
•
*Tomato and Parmesan
Focaccia*
(page 105)
•
Hazelnut Shortbread
(page 57)
•

When ruby grapefruit are unavailable, substitute the yellow flesh variety. Sprinkle with a little sugar and broil (grill).
•

Parmesan Roulade with Smoked Salmon

PARMESAN ROULADE

3 oz (90 g) butter

½ cup (2 oz/60 g) all-purpose (plain) flour

2 cups (16 fl oz/500 ml) milk

¼ cup (1 oz/30 g) grated Parmesan cheese

4 eggs

FILLING

4 oz (125 g) soft cream cheese

2 tablespoons dill sprigs

grated peel (rind) ½ lemon

24 slices smoked salmon

MELT the butter in a medium saucepan. Add the flour and cook for 1 minute. Gradually add the milk and cook until boiling and thickened. Add the cheese and remove the pan from the heat.

Separate the eggs. Beat the egg whites until stiff. Gently fold the egg yolks and the beaten egg whites into the cheese sauce.

Spoon the mixture into a lined jelly (Swiss) roll pan and bake in a slow oven (325°F/170°C/Gas Mark 3) for 30–35 minutes or until firm to touch (the Roulade will still be light and fluffy).

Remove from oven. Turn the Roulade out onto a sheet of parchment (baking paper). Trim the sides of the Roulade to prevent cracking, then immediately roll up and allow to cool.

Gently unroll the cooled Roulade, spread with cream cheese and then sprinkle lightly with dill sprigs and lemon peel. Re-roll and serve sliced with smoked salmon.

Serves 6

M • E • N • U

•

Tarte à L'Oignon
(page 97)

•

Parmesan Roulade with
Smoked Salmon

•

Apple Galettes
(page 11)

•

Make the Roulade slightly ahead of time and cut into slices before the guests arrive — ensure you cover the Roulade well to prevent it from drying out.

•

Pesto and Parmesan Palmiers

PESTO
1 bunch fresh basil leaves
2 cloves garlic
2 tablespoons pine nuts, toasted
½ cup (4 fl oz/125 ml) extra virgin
    olive oil

2 tablespoons freshly grated Italian
    Parmesan cheese
2 sheets of ready made puff pastry

PLACE the basil, garlic and pine nuts in a blender. Blend until smooth. Gradually add the oil in a very thin stream as you blend. Add the cheese and blend only until mixed through. Transfer to a bowl and refrigerate with plastic (cling) wrap placed directly on the surface of the Pesto.

Roll the pastry out a little more to form a rectangle. Spread Pesto thinly over the pastry, leaving a ¾ inch (2 cm) border around the outside of the dough. With one of the shorter sides of the pastry facing you, fold both sides in halfway towards the middle of the pastry, then fold both sides in again so both edges meet in the middle of the pastry. Then fold the pastry in half where the two edges meet (resulting in a long piece of pastry 6 layers thick).

Trim the ends off the pastry, then cut the pastry into ½ inch (1½ cm) thick slices. Place on greased baking sheets, cover and chill for 30 minutes.

Bake at 425°F (220°C/Gas Mark 7) for 12–15 minutes or until crisp and golden. Allow the palmiers to cool slightly, then transfer to a wire rack to cool thoroughly. Serve with remaining Pesto.

Makes about 18

M • E • N • U
•
Pineapple Slices with Mint
•
Pesto and Parmesan Palmiers
•
Truffle Eggs
(page 107)
•
Fresh pineapple with mint is a wonderful stimulant for the palate. Serve it on large platters.
•

Poached Trout with Dill Mayonnaise

2 fresh trout fillets, approx 2 lb
(1 kg), scaled
3 cups (24 fl oz/750 ml) strong-
tasting fresh fish stock (this
can be made from the bones of
the fish)
1 lemon, sliced

DILL MAYONNAISE
2 egg yolks
1 teaspoon lemon juice
½ cup (4 fl oz/125 ml) light
olive oil
2 teaspoons hot strong-tasting fresh
fish stock
2 tablespoons fresh dill, chopped

M • E • N • U
•
Stilton-filled Quail Eggs
(page 89)
•
Poached Trout with Dill
Mayonnaise
•
Tarte Tatin
(page 99)
•

USING a pair of tweezers, remove all the bones from the trout fillets. Place the fillets in a large frying pan and pour over the stock, making sure both fillets are covered. Heat the stock until almost boiling, then reduce the heat and cook for about 10–15 minutes or until the fillets are just cooked (do not overcook). Remove the pan from the heat, add the lemon and allow the fish to cool in the stock.

To make the Dill Mayonnaise, place the egg yolks in a blender and blend until pale and thick. With the motor still running add the lemon juice and then the oil in a very slow, steady stream — this process will take 5 minutes. Add the stock and dill and blend until well combined.

Lift the trout from the pan and serve with the Dill Mayonnaise and extra lemon if desired.

Serves 2–4

Queen Style Pudding

10 slices spicy fruit loaf, crusts
removed
½ cup (4 oz/125 g) Strawberry
Jam (page 39)
1½ cups (12 fl oz/375 ml) warm
milk

2 tablespoons (1½ fl oz/45 ml)
strawberry liqueur
2 eggs plus 4 eggs, separated
1 cup (3½ oz/100 g) superfine
(caster) sugar

SPREAD jam over one side of each slice of bread. Cut the bread into
½–¾ inch (1–2 cm) dice. Place the bread in 4 well-greased 1 cup
(8 fl oz/250 ml) capacity shallow ceramic baking dishes.

In a bowl mix together the milk, liqueur, 2 whole eggs, 4 egg yolks and
half the sugar. Pour this custard over the bread and leave to stand for
10 minutes. Bake in a moderate oven (350°F/180°C/Gas Mark 4) for
25 minutes.

Beat the egg whites until stiff. Gradually add the remaining sugar and
continue beating until very stiff and glossy. Pipe over the puddings to
form peaks on top. Return the puddings to the oven and bake a further
15 minutes or until the meringue is golden. Serve immediately.

Serves 6

M • E • N • U
•
Toasted Pecan Nut Muesli
with Maple Syrup
(page 101)
•
Smoked Ham Quiche
(page 85)
•
Queen Style Pudding
•
Cappuccino
•
This winter menu is
delicious on a cold
morning.
•

Red Salmon and Avocado Mousse

BASIC MOUSSE
¾ oz (20 g) gelatin
¼ cup (2 fl oz/60 ml) water
24 oz (750 g) Crème Fraiche
    (page 19)
1 cup (8 fl oz/250 ml) heavy
    (double) cream, whipped

2 egg whites, beaten until stiff
8 oz (250 g) salmon, freshly poached
½ teaspoon lemon pepper seasoning
2 ripe, unbruised avocados
1 lemon, juiced and strained
smoked salmon, for serving
Melba toasts, for serving

M • E • N • U
•
*Red Salmon and Avocado
Mousse*
•
*Duck with Citrus Sauce
(page 41)*
•
Fresh Raspberries
•

TO MAKE the mousse, first combine the gelatin and water and dissolve over simmering water or in the microwave. Combine the Crème Fraiche, cream and egg whites and then carefully add the gelatin. Divide this mixture evenly between two bowls.

Purée the salmon and add to one bowl of Crème Fraiche mixture with the lemon pepper. Push the avocado through a fine sieve, combine with the lemon juice, then add to the other bowl of mixture. Stir each mixture thoroughly and check seasonings.

Spoon the salmon mousse into a well-greased 6 cup (48 fl oz/1¾ L) mold. Smooth the top of the mousse. Carefully spoon the avocado mousse on top, making sure the mixtures stay separate (if it is hot day, refrigerate the salmon mixture for 10 minutes first). Cover and refrigerate for at least 2–3 hours.

Unmold the mousse and garnish with smoked salmon, serve with Melba toasts.

Serves 6

Salmon Gravlax with Caper Tapenade Style Sauce

SALMON GRAVLAX
1 lb (500 g) salmon fillet
2 teaspoons sea salt
1 tablespoon sugar
dill sprigs

TAPENADE
¾ cup (3½ oz/100 g) large black
   olives, pitted

1 teaspoon capers
2 anchovy fillets
¼ cup (2 oz/60 g) sun-dried
   tomatoes
¼ cup (2 fl oz/60 ml) olive oil

M • E • N • U
•
Sliced Bananas with
Shredded Fresh Coconut
•
Salmon Gravlax with
Caper Tapenade Style
Sauce
•
Cherry Muffins
(page 25)
•

USING a pair of tweezers, remove any visible bones from the salmon. Place the salmon skin side down in a shallow container, allowing the fillet to sit flat. Sprinkle the salmon with salt and sugar and a few sprigs of dill.

Cover with plastic (cling) wrap and place a few heavy cans or weights on top. Refrigerate for at least 2–3 days.

Place the olives, capers, anchovies and tomatoes in a blender. Blend until smooth (you may need to stir the mixture a few times to purée it successfully). With the motor running, add the oil in a thin steady stream, allowing the tapenade to thicken as it blends.

Serve the Gravlax very thinly sliced with the skin removed, accompanied by the Tapenade.

Serves 2

Scallop Gratin with Tomato Salsa

1 lb (500 g) scallop meat
  with coral (roe)
1 cup (8 fl oz/250 ml) strong-tasting
  fresh seafood stock
½ cup (4 fl oz/125 ml) light
  (single) cream
2 eggs
seasonings, to taste

¾ cup (3½ oz/100 g) cheese, grated
TOMATO SALSA
2 ripe vine-ripened tomatoes
2 French shallots
½ ripe, unbruised avocado
6 Niçoise olives, pitted
1 lemon, juiced
freshly ground black pepper, to taste

REMOVE the coral from the scallop and reserve. Cut off and discard any membranes or brown bits of scallop. In a saucepan bring the stock to a boil; pour ¾ over the scallop meat and the remainder over the coral. Allow to cool.

Drain the scallops and pureé in a blender or food processor. Combine the purée, whole drained scallop coral, cream, eggs and seasonings. Pour into 2 well-greased 1½ cup (12 fl oz/375 ml) gratin dishes. Sprinkle with cheese.

Place the gratin dishes in a baking dish and add sufficient hot water so it reaches halfway up the sides of the dishes. Bake in a moderate oven (350°F/180°C/Gas Mark 4) for 20 minutes or until firm. Remove from the oven and waterbath and cool to room temperature.

Finely chop the tomatoes, French shallots, avocado and olives. Toss together with the lemon juice and pepper. Serve as an accompaniment to the gratin.

Serves 2–4

M • E • N • U
•
Crudité Sticks
•
*Scallop Gratin with
Tomato Salsa*
•
*Fresh Fruit Poached in
Sauterne Syrup (page 51)*
•
Crudite sticks can be
prepared a couple of
hours in advance.
Choose a variety of
vegetables, such as
carrots, cucumber, celery,
cherry tomatoes and bell
peppers (capsicum).
•

Smoked Ham Quiche

PASTRY

2 cups (8 oz/250 g) all-purpose
(plain) flour

4 oz (125 g) butter, chilled
and diced

1 egg

iced water, as required

SMOKED HAM FILLING

3 leeks, finely chopped

2 tablespoons olive oil

4 eggs

½ cup (4 fl oz/125 ml) light (single)
cream

½ cup (2½ oz/75 g) Mozzarella or
smoked Mozzarella cheese, grated

2 tablespoons chopped chives

6½ oz (200 g) smoked ham, finely
shredded

freshly grated black pepper

¼ cup (1½ oz/45 g) Pecorino
cheese, grated

M • E • N • U

•

Butterscotch Pancakes
(page 17)

•

Smoked Ham Quiche

•

Fruit Jelly
(page 53)

•

PLACE the flour in a food processor. Add the butter and process until combined. Add the egg and sufficient water to form a smooth, manageable dough. Knead the dough lightly on a floured board, then wrap in plastic (cling) wrap and refrigerate for 30 minutes.

On a floured board roll the pastry into a circle large enough to line a 9½ inch (24 cm) fluted flan pan. When the pastry is large enough, carefully lift it into the greased pan and trim the edges. Place the pie crust in the freezer until required.

Sauté the leeks in oil over a very low heat for 10 minutes or until the leeks begin to caramelize without browning. Whisk the eggs and cream together. Add the Mozzarella, chives, ham, pepper and leeks. Spoon this mixture into the pie crust and sprinkle with the Pecorino cheese. Bake in a moderate oven (350°F/180°C/Gas Mark 4) for 40 minutes or until the filling is firm and the pastry is crisp. Serve hot or cold.

Serves 4–6

Smoked Trout and Pine Nut Salad

1 smoked trout
4 cups (12 oz/375 g) assorted lettuce
    leaves or mescalin (eg radicchio,
    green oakleaf, lambs tongue, baby
    endive, watercress, mustard cress,
    baby cos, witloof, red witloof,
    snow pea (mangetout) sprouts,
    rocket, mazuma etc)
2 small bocconcini cheese, sliced
2 tablespoons (1½ fl oz/45 ml) extra
    virgin olive oil
3 slices Italian bread, cubed
¼ cup (1 oz/30 g) pine nuts
4 small bantam eggs
DRESSING
2 fl oz (60 ml/¼ cup) extra virgin
    olive oil
2 tablespoons (1½ fl oz/45 ml)
    lemon juice
1 teaspoon balsamic vinegar

M • E • N • U
•
Smoked Trout and Pine
Nut Salad
•
Olive and Sun-dried
Tomato Bread
(page 67)
•
Chilled Mango Soufflé
(page 33)
•

REMOVE the head, skin and all bones from the trout, leaving two boneless fillets. Sort and wash the lettuce and arrange on a large plate. Flake the fish over the salad leaves and arrange bocconcini throughout the salad.

Heat the oil in a frying pan. Cook the bread cubes until golden on all sides; add to the salad. Toast the pine nuts in the same pan until golden and add to the salad. Fry the eggs and place on top of the salad.

Combine the dressing ingredients in a screw top jar or dressing bottle. Pour over the salad just before serving.

Serves 4

Stilton-filled Quail Eggs

12 quail eggs
24 slices Lebanese cucumber, ½ inch
  (1 cm) thick

2 tablespoons sun-dried tomato paste
  (passato)
2 oz (60 g) stilton cheese

PLACE the eggs in a saucepan of hot tap water. Place on the stove, cover, bring to a boil and cook for 6–8 minutes. Drain the eggs and cool under running cold water. Peel the eggs and cut them in half lengthways. Remove the yolks, push through a very fine sieve and set aside.

Place the cucumber slices on a serving plate. Spoon a little tomato paste onto each cucumber slice, then sit a quail egg on each slice.

Cream stilton, then spoon a little into the hollow of each egg. Top with the sieved egg yolk.

Makes 24

M · E · N · U

•

Stilton-filled Quail Eggs

•

Wild Mushroom in Paprika
(page 109)

•

Apricot Almond Cake
(page 13)

•

Cook the quail eggs in
advance as this can be a
fiddly job first thing
in the morning.

•

Strawberries in Strawberry Liqueur

PRALINE
½ cup (2¾ oz/80 g) almonds
⅔ cup (5 oz/150 g) sugar
¼ cup (2 fl oz/60 ml) water

LIQUEUR STRAWBERRIES
12 oz (375 g) strawberries
3½ oz (100 g) mixed red and white
  alpine strawberries, if available
1 cup (8 fl oz/250 ml) strawberry
  liqueur

M • E • N • U
•
Toasted Polenta with
Cheese
(page 103)
•
Molded Eggs Florentine
(page 63)
•
Strawberries in Strawberry
Liqueur
•
Strong Black Coffee
•

ROAST the nuts in a moderate oven (350°F/180°C/Gas Mark 4) for 10 minutes or until just golden. Place on a non-stick baking sheet.

Heat the sugar and water in a heavy based saucepan, stirring constantly until the sugar dissolves. Brush some water around the sides of the saucepan to remove any excess sugar crystals, then cook the syrup, without stirring, until it looks like toffee (this takes about 5 minutes, but do not leave it alone as the time can vary considerably).

Pour the toffee over the nuts and allow to harden and cool. Crush the praline to a fine powder in a food processor or blender.

Stem (hull) the strawberries and remove any that are bruised or marked. Pour over the strawberry liqueur and allow to stand for 10–30 minutes. Serve strawberries with or without the liqueur, sprinkled with the praline.

Serves 2–4

Sun-dried Bell Pepper (Capsicum) Tartlets

PASTRY

4 oz (125 g) butter, chilled and diced

1¾ oz (50 g) sun-dried bell pepper (capsicum)

2 cups (8 oz/250 g) all-purpose (plain) flour

1 teaspoon dried basil leaves

iced water, as required

FILLING

2 eggs

½ cup (4 fl oz/125 ml) light (single) cream

3½ oz (100 g) sun-dried bell pepper (capsicum), sliced

1 tablespoon chopped fresh basil or Pesto (page 73)

1 bunch chives

M • E • N • U

•

Fresh Mangoes

•

Oysters with Bacon and Fish Jelly
(page 69)

•

Sun-dried Bell Pepper (Capsicum) Tartlets

•

CREAM the butter and bell pepper together in a blender or food processor until smooth. Add the flour and basil and process until combined. Add sufficient water to form a manageable dough. Knead lightly on a floured board, then wrap in plastic (cling) wrap and refrigerate for 30 minutes.

Roll out the pastry and use to line 4 individual (4–5 inch/10–12 cm) fluted flan pans. Put the flan pans on a baking sheet and place in the freezer until required.

Combine the eggs, cream, bell pepper and basil. Spoon into the prepared flan pans. Arrange the chives in a lattice (criss cross) pattern over the top of the filling. Trim the edges so the chives fit within the pie crust.

Bake in a moderate oven (350°F/180°C/Gas Mark 4) for 25–30 minutes or until the filling is set and the pastry is crisp.

Serves 4

Tapenade Swirled Scones

TAPENADE

¾ cup (3½ oz/100 g) large, black
    olives, pitted

1 teaspoon capers

2 anchovy fillets

¼ cup (2 oz/60 g) sun-dried
    tomatoes

¼ cup (2 fl oz/60 ml) olive oil

SCONE DOUGH

1½ cups (6 oz/180 g) self-rising
    (raising) flour

2 oz (60 g) butter

1 cup (8 fl oz/250 ml) buttermilk or
    milk

2 tablespoons (1½ fl oz/45 ml)
    buttermilk, to glaze

1 egg yolk, to glaze

PLACE the olives, capers, anchovies and tomatoes in a blender or food processor. Blend until smooth. With the motor running, add the oil in a thin steady stream, allowing the tapenade to thicken as it blends.

Sift the flour into a bowl. With your fingertips, rub the butter into the flour. Add the buttermilk and mix to form a manageable dough. Lightly knead the scone dough on a floured board until it is smooth. Roll out the dough to form a rectangle that is ¾ inch (1½ cm) thick. Spread the Tapenade over the scone dough, leaving a 1 inch (2 cm) border. Roll up the dough, starting from one of the longer sides.

Cut the dough into 1 inch (2 cm) slices. Place the scones very close together on a greased baking sheet. Mix the buttermilk and egg yolk together and brush over the tops of the scones. Bake in a fairly hot oven (425°F/220°C/Gas Mark 7) for 15–20 minutes or until the scones are golden and cooked through.

Makes 10–12 scones

M • E • N • U
•
Peaches Marinated in a Sugar Syrup with Cloves
•
Tapenade Swirled Scones
•
Marinate either fresh, canned or dried peaches in advance and serve well chilled. Bake the scones in the oven while eating the peaches and have them hot straight from the oven.
•

Tarte à L'Oignon

RICH PASTRY
4 oz (125 g) butter
4 oz (125 g) cream cheese
1 cup (4 oz/125 g) all-purpose
    (plain) flour
pinch salt

8 onions, very thinly sliced
¼ cup (2 fl oz/60 ml) olive oil
2 tablespoons (1½ oz/45 g) butter
2 eggs
½ cup (4 fl oz/125 ml) milk
freshly ground pepper, to taste

BEAT the butter and cream cheese together in a food processor or blender until smooth. Add the flour and salt and process until a manageable dough forms (add a little extra flour if necessary). Transfer to a lightly floured board and knead lightly until smooth. Cover with plastic (cling) wrap and refrigerate for 30 minutes.

Roll out the pastry and use it to fill an 8 inch (20 cm) flan pan. Freeze until required.

Sauté the onions in oil and butter over a very low heat for 15 minutes or until the onions have caramelized. In a bowl, whisk together the eggs, milk and pepper.

Arrange the onions in the pie crust then pour over the custard. Bake in a moderate oven (350°F/180°C/Gas Mark 4) for 25 minutes or until the custard has set and pastry is crisp. Serve hot or cold.

Serves 4–6

M • E • N • U
•
Poached Fruit
•
Tarte à L'Oignon
•
Chilled Mango Soufflé
(page 33)
•
Lemon Tea
•

Tarte Tatin

PECAN PASTRY

½ cup (1 ¾ oz/50 g) ground
    pecan nuts

1 cup (4 oz/125 g) all-purpose
    (plain) flour

½ cup (3 ½ oz/100 g) superfine
    (caster) sugar

1 tablespoon (1 ½ oz/45 g) butter

1 egg yolk

iced water, as required

FILLING

2 ½ oz (75 g) butter

½ cup (3 ½ oz/100 g) superfine
    (caster) sugar

4 golden delicious apples, peeled,
    cored and cut into eighths

1 tablespoon Calvados

M • E • N • U

•

Fresh Fruit Platter

•

Champagne

•

Scallop Gratin with
Tomato Salsa
(page 83)

•

Tarte Tatin

•

PLACE the nuts, flour and sugar in a food processor or blender and process to combine. Add the butter and egg yolk, then sufficient water to form a manageable dough. Lightly knead on a floured board, cover with plastic (cling) wrap and refrigerate for 30 minutes.

Melt the butter in a frying pan with a metal or ovenproof handle (if an ovenproof frying pan is unavailable, use a heavy cake pan). Add the sugar and stir to dissolve. Place the apples in the syrup and cook over a low heat for 10 minutes or until they are caramelized, turning occasionally. Arrange the apples in a circular pattern.

Roll out the pastry to fit the bottom of the frying pan. Place the pastry on top of the apples and bake in moderate oven (350°F/180°C/Gas Mark 4) for 15–20 minutes or until the pastry is golden and cooked through. Cool in the pan before inverting onto a plate to serve.

Serves 4

Toasted Pecan Nut Muesli with Maple Syrup

½ cup (2½ oz/75 g) rolled oats
¼ cup (¼ oz/40 g) bran flakes
1 tablespoon maple syrup
2 tablespoons oatbran
1 tablespoon wheat germ
2 teaspoons lecithin, optional
½ cup (3 oz/90 g) pecans

½ cup (3 oz/90 g) dried apricots, sliced
½ cup (3 oz/90 g) sun-dried golden raisins (sultanas)
chopped fresh fruit (eg banana, apple etc)
yogurt, for serving
maple syrup, for serving

THOROUGHLY combine the oats, bran flakes and maple syrup. Spread in a thin layer on a baking sheet. Bake at 350°F (180°C/Gas Mark 4) for 10 minutes or until the oats and bran flakes have dried. Cool on the baking sheet.

Combine the toasted grains with the oatbran, wheat germ, lecithin, pecans, apricots, and golden raisins. Serve in large bowls topped with fresh fruit, yogurt and maple syrup.

Serves 2

M • E • N • U
•
Toasted Pecan Nut Muesli with Maple Syrup
•
Brioche with Poached Eggs (page 15)
•
Dried Muscatel Grapes Marinaded in Grape Juice
•
Serve the muesli in large bowls with jugs of maple syrup.
•

Toasted Polenta with Cheese

1 cup (8 fl oz/250 ml) strong-tasting
   fresh chicken stock
½ cup (3 oz/90 g) polenta
   (fine corn meal)
1 teaspoon seeded mustard
sea salt, to taste

2 tablespoons (1½ oz/45 g) butter
1 tablespoon olive oil
½ cup (4 fl oz/125 ml) light (single)
   cream
½ cup (2½ oz/75 g) grated
   vintage cheddar cheese

PLACE the stock in a saucepan and bring to a boil. Add the polenta, mustard and salt. Cook for 3–4 minutes or until all the liquid has been absorbed. Pour the polenta into a non-stick 12 x 8 inch (30 x 20 cm) pan. Cool, then remove from the pan and cut into squares.

Heat the butter and oil in a frying pan. Cook the polenta squares until golden on all sides. Pour over the cream and cheese; heat through until the cream boils and the cheese melts. Serve hot.

Serves 4

M • E • N • U
•
Fresh Fruit
•
*Toasted Polenta with
Cheese*
•
*Duck with Citrus Sauce
(page 41)*
•
*Serve platters of fruit
already split open.*
•

Tomato and Parmesan Focaccia

¾ oz (20 g) compressed yeast

½ teaspoon sugar

½ teaspoon sea salt, or to taste

2 tablespoons olive oil

1 cup (8 fl oz/250 ml) warm water

3 cups (8 oz/250 g) unbleached all-purpose (plain) flour

¼ cup (1 oz/30 g) grated Parmesan cheese

3 fl oz (90 ml) olive oil, extra

1 ripe vine-ripened tomato, thinly sliced

1 teaspoon sea salt flakes

CREAM the yeast, sugar, salt and oil. Add the water and half the flour to the yeast mixture. Beat until smooth, cover and place in a warm position for 40 minutes or until the mixture is doubled in size.

Knock down the dough, make a well in the middle and into this add the remaining flour, Parmesan and half the oil. Knead the dough on a floured board for 10 minutes or until the mixture is smooth.

Roll the dough out to form a large rectangle, approximately 1 inch (2 cm) thick. Lift the dough onto a baking sheet that has been thoroughly greased with olive oil. Prick the dough all over with a fork, brush it with oil and arrange the tomato slices over the top. Brush remaining oil over the tomatoes, and sprinkle with salt flakes. Lightly cover the dough and place in a warm position for 40 minutes or until it has doubled in size.

Bake in a hot oven (400°F/200°C/Gas Mark 6) for 35–40 minutes or until the focaccia is golden on top and cooked through, covering the tomatoes with foil if they begin to burn.

Serves 4

M • E • N • U
•
Tomato and Parmesan Focaccia
•
Antipasto (Marinated Vegetables, Cheeses, Cooked Meats)
•
Figs in Port with Mascarpone (page 45)
•
Serve the focaccia with antipasto on large bread boards.
•

Truffle Eggs

6 eggs
½ cup (4 fl oz/125 ml) heavy
    (double) cream
2 tablespoons (1½ oz/45 g) butter

1 teaspoon truffle oil (optional)
6 black or white truffles, thinly sliced
4 slices bread, toasted

IN A bowl, whisk the eggs and cream together. Gently heat the butter and oil in a heavy-based frying pan. Pour in the egg mixture and sprinkle over the truffle slices (use more truffle slices if desired). Allow the base of the egg to begin to set, then with a flat-topped wooden spoon gently pull the cooked egg into the middle of the pan, so the uncooked portion reaches the bottom of the pan. Continue this process until the eggs are just cooked and not too firm.

Lift the eggs onto the toast and serve immediately.

Serves 2

M • E • N • U
•
Paté de Foie Gras
•
Truffle Eggs
•
*Fresh Fruit Poached in
Sauterne Syrup
(page 51)*
•

Wild Mushroom in Paprika

1 lb (500 g) assorted fresh wild
    mushrooms (eg shiitake, woodear,
    pine, cepes, oyster, Swiss brown,
    field mushrooms, chanterelle,
    morels)
2 tablespoons (1½ oz/45 g) butter

2 tablespoons (1½ fl oz/45 ml)
    olive oil
1–2 teaspoons good quality paprika
pinch saffron threads
toasted brioche slices (page 15), for
    serving

Sort through the mushrooms, discarding any that are damaged and wipe them over with a damp cloth.

Heat the butter and oil in a heavy frying pan. Add the paprika and saffron and cook gently for 1 minute or until very fragrant. Add the mushrooms and cook for 4–5 minutes or until they are tender, turning them occasionally.

Spoon the mushrooms onto warm brioche slices.

Serves 4

M • E • N • U
•
Cherry Muffins
(page 25)
•
Wild Mushroom in
Paprika
•
Brioche
(page 15)
•
Black, White and Red
Currants dusted with
Confectioners' (Icing)
Sugar
•

Index